Ballerina

The Dancing Class

by Anna Pavlova

illustrated with art by Edgar Degas

SIMON & SCHUSTER

London

Vivid are my earliest
recollections, which
take me back to the
time when I was living
in a little apartment
with my mother in
the city.

View of Saint-Valéry-sur-Somme

I was the only child; and my father having
died two years after my birth, we two were
alone in the world. We were very poor –
very poor indeed…

and yet my mother would never fail to provide on special occasions, a surprise for me, in the shape of some treat. I can still remember my enthusiasm when, on one birthday, I heard that we were to celebrate by going to see a performance at the theatre.

At the Milliner's

1882
degas

I had never yet been to the theatre, and I plied my mother with questions in order to find out what kind of show it was that we were going to see.

Three Dancers Preparing for Class (detail)

She replied by telling me the story of the
Sleeping Beauty – a favourite of mine
among all fairy tales, and one which she
had already told me countless times.

When we left for the theatre, I felt
unspeakably happy beside my mother, her
arm tenderly enclosing my waist.

"You are going to enter fairyland," she said,
as we were being whirled across the darkness
towards the theatre, that mysterious unknown.

The music of the *Sleeping Beauty* is by
the great Russian composer, Tchaikovsky.
As soon as the orchestra began to play,
I became very grave and attentive, eagerly
listening, moved for the first time in my
life by the call of Beauty.

But when the curtain
rose, displaying the
golden hall of a
wonderful palace,
I could not withhold
a shout of delight.

Dancer Onstage (detail)

And I remember hiding my face in my hands when the old hag appeared on the stage in her car driven by rats.

In the second act a swarm of youths and maidens appeared, and danced a most delightful waltz.

The Ballet from Robert le Diable (detail)

"How would you like to dance like that?" asked my mother with a smile.

"Oh," I replied, "I should prefer to dance as the pretty lady does who plays the part of the princess. One day I shall be the princess, and dance upon the stage of this very theatre."

Dancers, Pink and Green (detail)

My mother muttered that I was her silly little dear, and never suspected that I had just discovered the idea that was to guide me throughout my life.

Little Girl Practicing at the Bar
OVERLEAF: *The Dance Class* (detail)

When we left the theatre, I was living in a dream. During the journey home, I kept thinking of the day when I should make my first appearance on the stage, in the part of the Sleeping Beauty.

That very night, I dreamed that I was a ballerina, and spent my whole life dancing, like a butterfly, to the sounds of Tchaikovsky's lovely music.

I love to remember that night.

The Rehearsal Onstage (detail)

Anna Pavlova in La Fille Mal Gardée

About Anna Pavlova

Born poor in a suburb of St. Petersburg, Russia, Anna Pavlova (1881–1931) was
inspired to enter the ballet after seeing a performance of the *Sleeping Beauty* at
the Mariinsky Theatre with her mother. At the time, the public favoured athletic
Italian ballerinas, so young Anna's weak feet and scrawny body were not consid-
ered promising. However, after several years of practicing and waiting, Pavlova
was finally admitted to the Imperial Ballet School.

Upon graduation from the school, with much ingenuity and hard work,
Pavlova had begun transforming her weaknesses into gifts. She modified her

ballet shoes with leather and stitching to give herself greater stamina. (Today's ballet slippers are similar to those adapted by Pavlova). And she used her flexible body and delicate manner to give her performances an expressiveness that audiences loved.

Eventually, Pavlova became prima ballerina at the Mariinsky Theatre, fulfilling her childhood dream. She toured widely throughout the world – it has been said that she journeyed 350,000 miles to 4,000 cities in fifteen years – often performing her signature piece, "The Dying Swan".

In 1931, Pavlova contracted pleurisy, an inflammation of the lungs. Doctors could have saved her life with an operation that would have left her unable to perform, but Pavlova refused to live without dancing. Her last words were reportedly "Get my swan costume ready." The night after her death, at the theatre where she was to perform "The Dying Swan," the orchestra played, the curtain opened, and a spotlight went up on an empty stage.

About Edgar Degas

The French Impressionist artist Edgar Degas (1834–1917) created paintings, drawings, pastels, sculpture, and photographs. One of his favourite subjects was the ballet dancers of the Paris Opéra, who feature in about fifteen hundred of his works. Degas was as familiar with the discipline of the dancers' practice sessions as he was with the magic of their performances.

Self-portrait

Degas never worked with Anna Pavlova and they probably never met. It is possible that he saw her perform in Paris, but that would have been decades after he created most of his ballet-inspired art. Despite their separate histories, Degas's art and Pavlova's words reveal a shared passion: the mesmerizing spell of ballet.

This story is drawn from Anna Pavlova's 1922 autobiography, *Pages of My Life* (translated by Sebastien Voirol), published by Michel de Brunoff, Paris.

The photograph of Anna Pavlova inside this book (in *La Fille Mal Gardée*, from a program, 1910) and the photograph of Pavlova on the back cover (in "The Dying Swan," ca. 1910) are from the Theater Collection of the Museum of the City of New York. All other works of art reproduced in this book are by Edgar Degas (French, 1834–1917) and are in the collections of The Metropolitan Museum of Art, unless otherwise noted.

Dancers Practicing at the Bar

COVER: *Dancer in Green* (detail). Pastel on paper, 28 x 15 in., ca. 1883. Bequest of Joan Whitney Payson, 1975 1976.201.7 *The Dancing Class*. Oil on wood, 7¾ x 10⅝ in., probably 1871. H. O. Havemeyer Collection, Bequest of Mrs. H. O. Havemeyer, 1929 29.100.184 *View of Saint-Valéry-sur-Somme*. Oil on canvas, 20 x 24 in., 1896–98. Robert Lehman Collection, 1975 1975.1.167 *A Woman Ironing*. Oil on canvas, 21⅜ x 15½ in., 1873. H. O. Havemeyer Collection, Bequest of Mrs. H. O. Havemeyer, 1929 29.100.46 *At the Milliner's*. Pastel on pale gray wove paper, 30 x 34 in., 1882. H. O. Havemeyer Collection, Bequest of Mrs. H. O. Havemeyer, 1929 29.100.38 *Three Dancers Preparing for Class* (detail). Pastel on buff-colored wove paper, 21½ x 20½ in., after 1878. H. O. Havemeyer Collection, Bequest of Mrs. H. O. Havemeyer, 1929 29.100.558 *Dancer* (detail). Pastel, charcoal, and chalk on paper, 12½ x 19¼ in., ca. 1880. From the Collection of Walter H. and Leonore Annenberg. *The Singer in Green*. Pastel on light blue laid paper, 23¾ x 18¼ in., ca. 1884. Bequest of Stephen C. Clark, 1960 61.101.7 *The Violinist*, study for *The Dance Lesson*. Pastel and charcoal on green paper, 15⅛ x 11¼ in., ca. 1878–79. Rogers Fund, 1918 19.51.1 *Dancer Onstage* (detail). Gouache over graphite underdrawing on yellow paper, laid down on board, 7 x 9 in., ca. 1877. The Lesley and Emma Sheafer Collection, Bequest of Emma A. Sheafer, 1973 1974.356.30 *The Ballet from* Robert le Diable (detail). Oil on canvas, 26 x 21⅜ in., 1871. H. O. Havemeyer Collection, Bequest of Mrs. H. O. Havemeyer, 1929 29.100.552 *Dancers, Pink and Green* (detail). Oil on canvas, 32⅛ x 29¾ in., ca. 1890. H. O. Havemeyer Collection, Bequest of Mrs. H. O. Havemeyer, 1929 29.100.42 *Little Girl Practicing at the Bar*. Black chalk heightened with white chalk on pink laid paper, 12⅛ x 11½ in., ca. 1878–80. H. O. Havemeyer Collection, Bequest of Mrs. H. O. Havemeyer, 1929 29.100.943 *The Dance Class* (detail). Oil on canvas, 32¼ x 30¼ in., probably 1874. Bequest of Mrs. Harry Payne Bingham, 1986 1987.47.1 *The Rehearsal Onstage* (detail). Pastel over brush-and-ink drawing on cream-colored paper, laid down on bristol board and mounted on canvas, 21 x 28½ in., 1874. H. O. Havemeyer Collection, Bequest of Mrs. H. O. Havemeyer, 1929 29.100.39 *Self-portrait*. Oil on paper, laid down on canvas, 16 x 13½ in., possibly 1854. Bequest of Stephen C. Clark, 1960 61.101.6 *Dancers Practicing at the Bar*. Mixed media on canvas, 29¾ x 32 in., 1877. H. O. Havemeyer Collection, Bequest of Mrs. H. O. Havemeyer, 1929 29.100.34 BACK FLAP: *The Little Fourteen-Year-Old Dancer*. Bronze (partly tinted), cotton skirt, satin hair ribbon, wooden base, H. 37½ in., 1879–81, cast in 1922. H. O. Havemeyer Collection, Bequest of Mrs. H. O. Havemeyer, 1929 29.100.370

First published in Great Britain in 2001 by Simon & Schuster UK Ltd
Africa House, 64 - 78 Kingsway, London, WC2B 6AH

Copyright © 2001 by The Metropolitan Museum of Art

A CIP catalogue record for this book is available from the British Library upon request

ISBN 0 689 83647 3

Printed in Hong Kong

1 3 5 7 9 10 8 6 4 2

Produced by the Department of Special Publications, The Metropolitan Museum of Art:
Robie Rogge, Publishing Manager; William Lach, Editor; Anna Raff, Designer; Tatiana Ginsberg, Production Associate.
All photography by The Metropolitan Museum of Art Photograph Studio, except for photographs of Anna Pavlova, courtesy of the Museum of the City of New York.